Alexandra ~
Life is what you make of it!
Always dream!

Laugh out loud ~

Angie Raiff ☺

# Daydreaming Daze

## Silly Summer Poems

Written by Angie Raiff
Illustrated by Liz Raiff

Published by
Bear Lake Publishing
31914 Village Green Blvd.
Warrenville, IL 60055
(630) 836-0127

Text was set in Tempus Sans/Kirsten by Allegro Design Inc.

02  01  00  99    5  4  3  2  1

Library of Congress Catalog Card Number 98-93944

ISBN 0-9661132-1-7

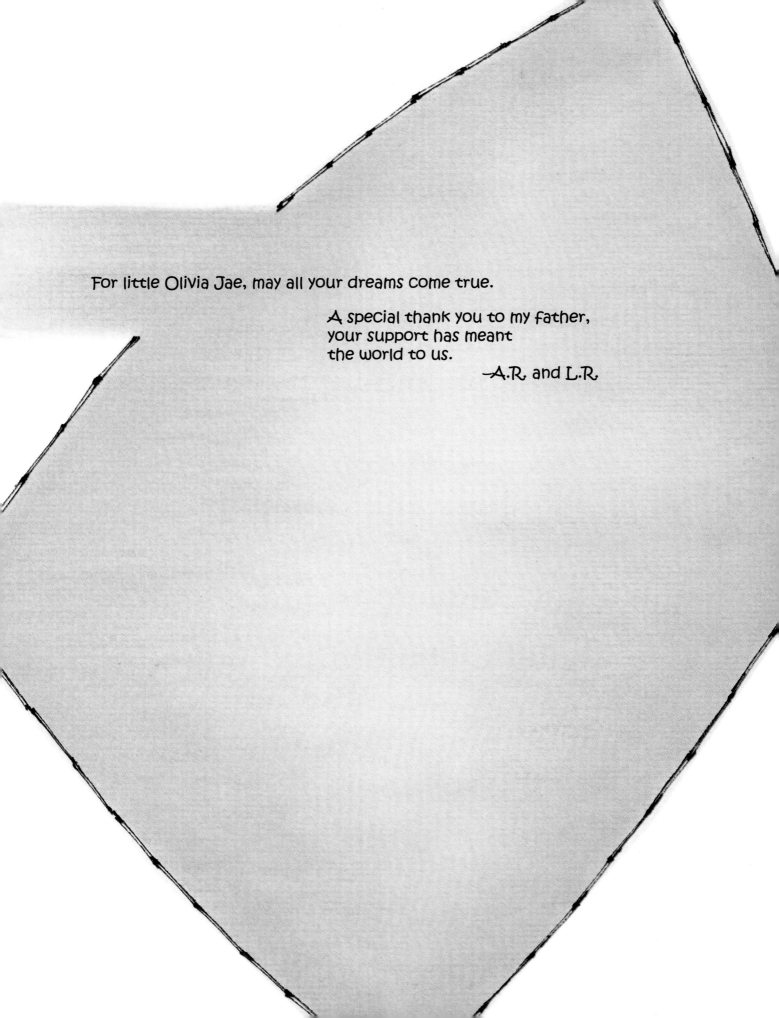

For little Olivia Jae, may all your dreams come true.

A special thank you to my father,
your support has meant
the world to us.

-A.R. and L.R.

# Daydream

Oh, how I've looked forward to summer this year.
A warm breeze, hot sun, birds chirping far and near.
With picnics and swimming . . . just so many things,
all the fun that summer brings.
I'll ride my bike and climb a tree.
How much fun summer is going to be.
The neighborhood kids will sell lemonade,
chase lightning bugs and have a parade.
I'd better get started, my list isn't small.
But right now I'll lay here and dream of it all.

# Anticipation of Vacation

It is summer time again.

The car is packed to go.

I promise I'll write and send

a postcard to you and Sally Joe.

We're going on vacation.

We've been packing for three days.

Mom and Dad need some relaxation,

and I need a new place to play.

# Gritty but Great

With sand in my bucket
and a shovel in my hand,
I'll build a big castle
and make it quite grand.

Mix water and sand
to pack it real tight.
I'll shape each wall
until it is just right.

The minutes have passed
and the hours have too.
I'm proud of my work.
How about you?

# Nature's Flavor

Put up our tent and settle in,

grab the canoe and let the fun begin.

We'll paddle along as the river bends,

catching fish until daylight ends.

Build a campfire and gather around,

listen closely for nature's sounds.

Can you hear the crickets' song?

We could almost sing along.

Other animals, big and small

are stirring, listen for their call.

We're glad our tent zips tight.

No creepy visitors wanted tonight!

# Gills and Thrills

Every year I travel far
and take my fishing pole
to a place called Bear Lake,
it is my favorite fishing hole.

Grandma spends her time
teaching me the way
to bait my hook, cast my line,
then sit and wait all day.

I am always very patient,
no matter how long it takes.
Watching very quietly,
for that fish to steal my bait.

# A Buzz in the Air

Yellow as the sunlight soaring through the air.
Black as the night giving children a scare.
Looking for a place to land-
Oh no, not on my hand!
Do you think anyone can see,
I'm running from a bumble bee?

There is a mosquito buzzing in my ear,
a bite from him is what I fear.
He's coming close, oh my—oh dear!
Ouch! He just bit me in the rear.
I won't sit down for a whole year.

## Spare Change

Today is the day we make a plan
to set up a lemonade stand.
Start with a box and a big white sign
"Lemonade For Sale-
Please Form One Line."
We've worked hard to mix it just right.
I even started stirring late last night.
10 cents, 2 nickels or 10 pennies is all.
Our cups are really quite small.
It's fresh and it's cold.
Three cups we have sold.
To mom who has stopped twice so far.
She even drove up once in her car.
"Is anybody thirsty? It's hot today!"
Oh well, tomorrow is a new day.

# Sweet Treat

Sunday is simple, it's vanilla for me.
On Monday I like cherries jubilee.
By Tuesday I choose bubble gum.
Wednesday is strawberry – yum, yum!
Come Thursday, I head for rocky road.
Friday is peppermint, by the truckload.
Saturday calls for chocolate chip.
Then Sunday, I start over and double dip.

# Ooooooh!

Today is the Fourth of July.
Colors dancing across the sky.
Blue, green and red so bright.
Such quick flashes of light.
We lay on a blanket or sit in a chair,
tilt our heads back, to the sky we stare.

# Ahhhhhhh!

Oh how I love the Fourth of July,
with the fireworks lighting up the sky.
Wow, a red one. Oh look, now blue.
What is a little kid to do?
I look to the left and I look to the right,
just so many awesome sights!

# Who Me?

Let's play a game, it will be fun.
I made it simple for everyone.
I'll give some clues to help you out,
while you decide who I am talking about . . .

I am quite large and easy to see,
except when something is blocking me.
I'm round in shape and give off a glow,
making those warm that live below.
If you haven't guessed, here's one more clue.
Look straight ahead, I'm staring at you.

You did it! You are right! I am the sun.
I make summer fun for everyone!

# Barefoot

That first step is so cool.
Reminds me of a dip in the pool.
What is it I feel,
under my heal?
I'll ask my big toe.
He will always know.
Than with a little wiggle,
followed by a silly jiggle.
It's grass your in.
Oh, let's step in it again.

# Watermelon Grin

When I eat the summer's juicy treat,
I am always covered from head to feet.
I use both hands and open wide,
but mom always makes me stand outside.
I take one bite, then two or three.
Is there any more watermelon for me?

# Stalk Talk

Here we stand, straight and tall.
It is hard to believe we started so small.
One by one and row by row,
the farmer helps us each to grow.
We go on for miles covering the ground,
like a blanket and barely making a sound.
Some have two ears and some have one.
Does it have anything to do with the sun?

# Amuse Me

Kids of all ages gather around
as the carnival rolls into town.
A ferris wheel and games galore,
it is everything you could hope for.

Cotton candy and sno-cones to eat.
Funny looking clowns with extra big feet.
Buy your tickets and get in line.
The carnival is here rain or shine.

# Sidewalk Sailing

With my new wheels under me,
I am alone and I feel free.
"Go Slow," I heard Dad say.
I could ride this bike all day.
Down the sidewalk I sail,
blazing my own trail.
"Honk! Honk! Out of my way!"
I have not learned to use the brake today.

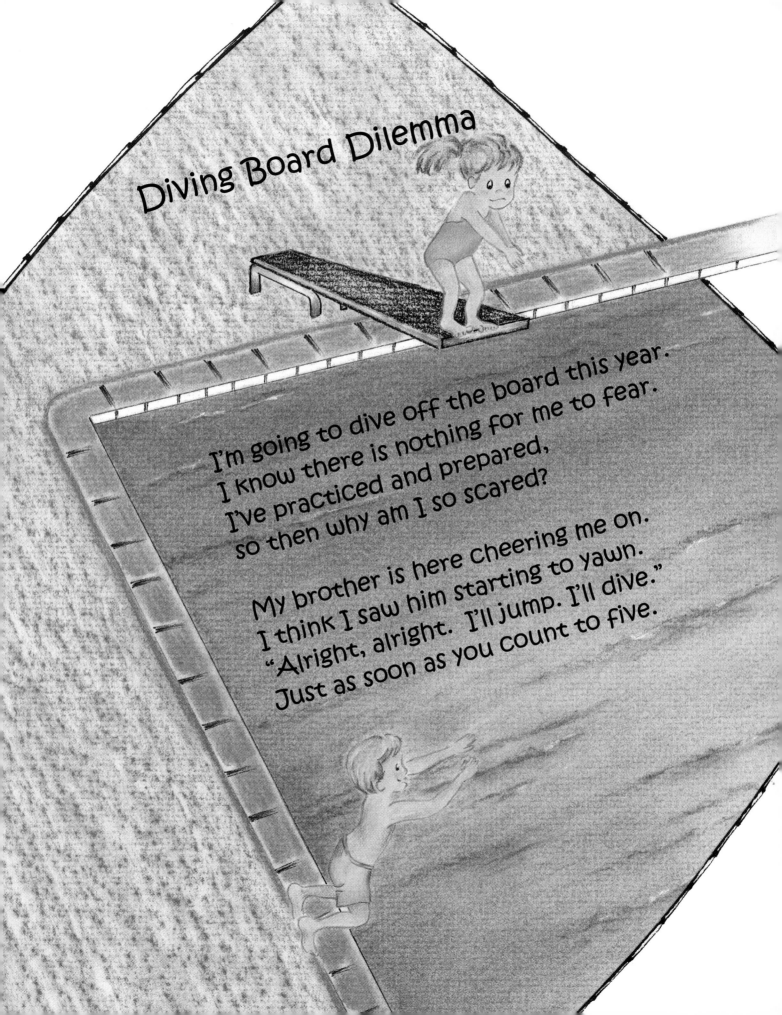

# Diving Board Dilemma

I'm going to dive off the board this year.
I know there is nothing for me to fear.
I've practiced and prepared,
so then why am I so scared?

My brother is here cheering me on.
I think I saw him starting to yawn.
"Alright, alright. I'll jump. I'll dive."
Just as soon as you count to five.

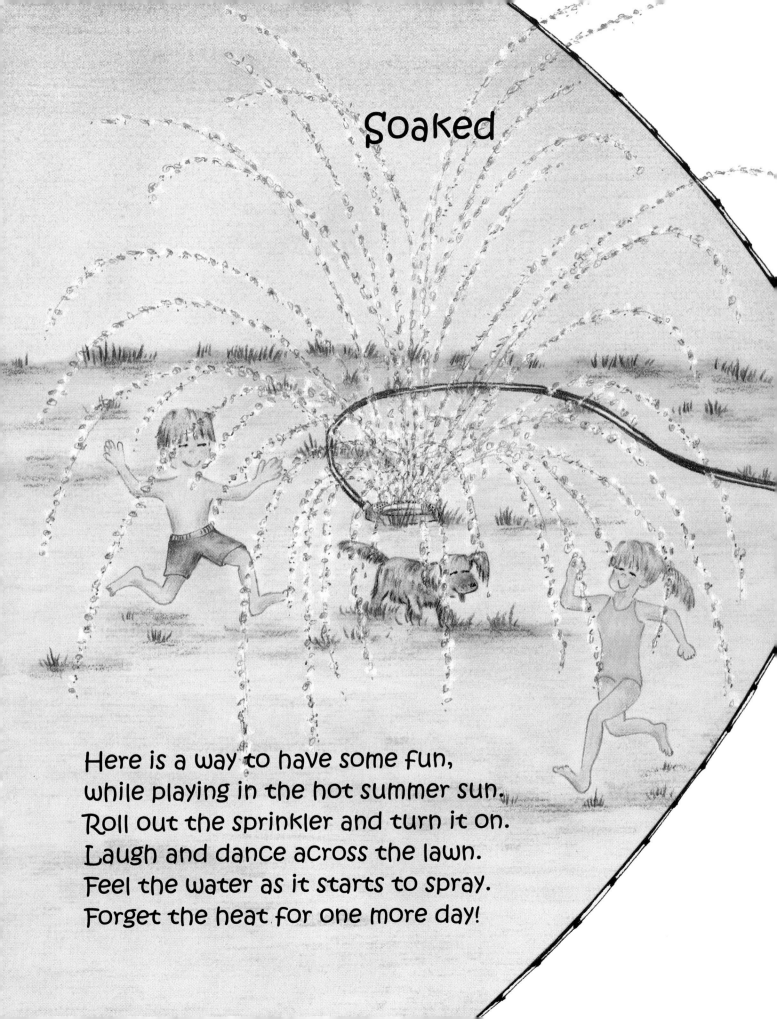

# Soaked

Here is a way to have some fun,
while playing in the hot summer sun.
Roll out the sprinkler and turn it on.
Laugh and dance across the lawn.
Feel the water as it starts to spray.
Forget the heat for one more day!

# County Fair Fun

Families come from all around
to celebrate summer
at the county fair grounds.
Homegrown veggies are ready for show.
Weather is perfect to enjoy
goodies everywhere you go.
The cows and pigs are fed just right.
The judges are ready.
Is there a blue ribbon in sight?

# Ahh . . . Summer

It's getting warm, it's getting hot.
Summer is here, winter is not.

I traded in my hat and coat,
for a swimsuit and a floating boat.

I can play outside, maybe stay up late.
No doubt about it, summer is great.

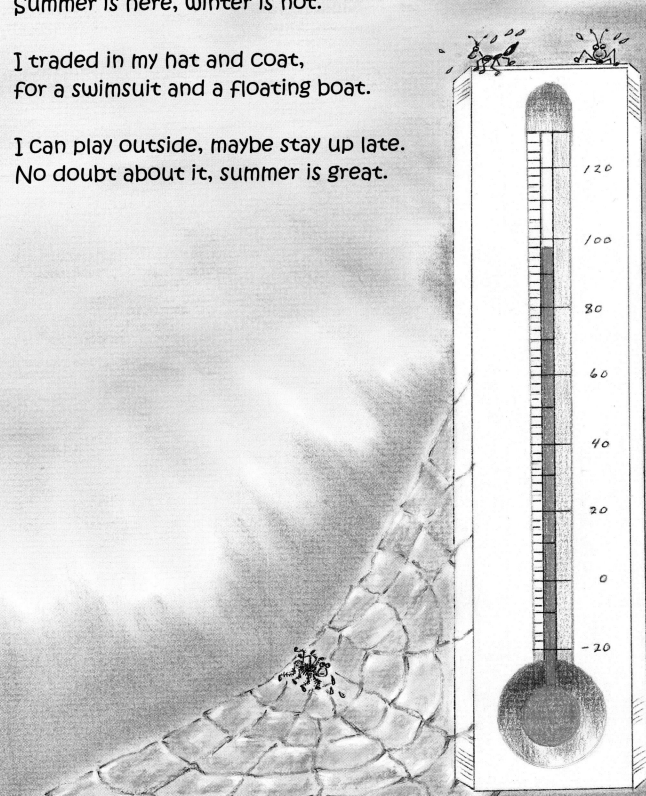

# Nightlights

In the dark of night,
the flash is so bright,
just enough light,
to get one in sight.

Would you like to catch a firefly?
It is very easy, just give it a try.
First, you spot one with your eye.
Open your hands, be very sly.
We've had our fun now, you and I.
Time to set them free—bye, bye.

# Bored

Mom, I'm bored,
there is nothing to do.
I've played with my toys
and my stuffed animals too.
I need a new game,
a new toy, a new plan,
Something to pass the time,
around the house I already ran.
I could twiddle my thumbs
and watch the grass grow.
Set the table for you?
How did I know!

# Think
# Your Way There

Have you ever wanted to
travel and see great sights?
But, you have no money and
Mom tuck's you in at night.

You can go everywhere
that you want to go.
It will be your secret,
no one would know.

A swim through the ocean
with a dolphin as your guide.
Set your thoughts into
motion with an airplane ride.

Take a journey into space
where the stars are your friends.
Walk in the desert
where the sand never ends.

The world is waiting,
take a step and fall in.
Just open a book and
let your adventure begin.

# Bummer, No More Summer

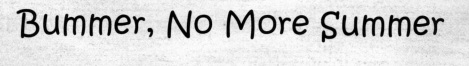

My how time flies by,
it was just the Fourth of July.
I had a blast, it sure was fun,
being silly in the summer sun.
I sold lemonade, ate ice cream galore,
jumped off the diving board and much, much more.
The fun won't stop because school is near;
ring the bell, open the doors, it's finally here.
New books, new pencils and even new friends.
I can't wait to have homework again . . .
                                        I think!